After School Adventures

(Activities for Latch-Key Programs, Child Care Centers, Classrooms, Recreational Programs, and Home)

by
Harriet Kinghorn
Lillian Dudley
Nancy L. Reed

Cover and Inside Illustrations by
Kris Tierney

Publishers
T.S. Denison and Company, Inc.
Minneapolis, Minnesota 55431

ACKNOWLEDGMENTS

We would like to thank Diane Fusoro for the preparation of the manuscript. Michael Morris for the preparation of the music, and Brad and Ben Boesiger for their help with the games.

Standard Book Number: 513-02187-6
After School Adventures
Copyright © 1993 by T.S. Denison and Company, Inc.
9601 Newton Avenue South
Minneapolis, Minnesota 55431

INTRODUCTION

After School Adventures provides after-school and out-of-school activities which can be used in classrooms, recreation centers, child-care centers, latch-key programs and even at home.

After School Adventures is divided into seven categories: Art, Games, Drama, Music and Movement, Hodgepodge, Nutritious Snacks, and Sidewalk Careers.

The **ART** section has suggestions for working with different media as well as a page of "recipes for art projects."

The **GAMES** section contains indoor and outdoor games for all ages and for any number of players.

The **DRAMA** section includes plays for children to perform. This section also includes pantomime activities, easy puppetry, and play starters.

The **MUSIC and MOVEMENT** section includes movement activities and musical expression activities. Although many of these activities include music, they can be conducted as movement activities without music.

The **HODGEPODGE** section provides a wide range of activities utilizing a variety of easily obtainable objects.

The **NUTRITIOUS SNACKS** section provides recipes that each child can make individually and eat.

The **SIDEWALK CAREERS** section includes creative sidewalk activities that allow children to learn more about a variety of interesting careers.

The activities in this book can be adapted to varying lengths of time. When appropriate, extension activities are suggested. The variety of activities in this resource will provide enjoyable and creative experiences for both you and your children.

CONTENTS

Section 1 - ART

COLLAGE

A collage is a design or picture that is made by gluing pieces of paper or other materials onto another surface.

MATERIALS: Various colors of construction paper scraps, glue, scissors, crayons or markers, a large background sheet of paper, books that contain collages such as by Leo Lionne, and an encyclopedia with an entry on *Collage*.

DIRECTIONS:
1. Look at photographs of collages that have been created by professional artists.
2. Discuss the designs and colors of the collages.
3. Make a collage of your own by gluing paper on a background to create a design or picture.

EXTENSION: Tell or write a story about your collage.

FOIL DRAWINGS

MATERIALS: Cardboard, foil, rounded toothpick, string, tape.

DIRECTIONS:
1. Wrap a piece of foil around a piece of cardboard. Try not to wrinkle the foil.
2. With a toothpick, draw a design or picture on the foil. You can use the toothpick to draw solid lines or to make lines of dots. Try not to tear the foil.
3. Draw a design on the edges of the foil to frame your picture.
4. Make a hanger for your foil drawing by taping two ends of a 2" - 3" piece of string to the back of the drawing. The hanger should not show above the top of the drawing.

EXTENSION: Write what you were thinking about as you created your picture. Title your foil drawing.

MOBILE

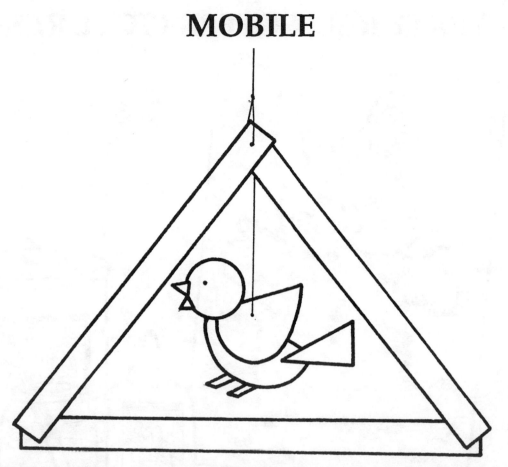

MATERIALS: Strips of tagboard (1/2" x 12"), various colors of construction paper, stapler, glue, scissors, pencil, needle, white thread.

DIRECTIONS:
1. Staple three strips of tagboard together to form a triangle.
2. Use construction paper to create an object or an animal to hang inside the triangle. You may want to draw the object on the construction paper before you begin to cut it out. Use different colors for the different parts of the object. Glue all the parts together.
3. Hang your object or animal in the center of the triangle using a needle and thread.
4. Attach one end of a 12" length of thread to the top of the triangle. Attach the other end of the thread to a paper clip which may be used to hang the mobile.

EXTENSION: List as many words as possible that describe motion.

TEXTURED COFFEE PICTURES

MATERIALS: Tagboard, dried and used coffee grounds, paint made by mixing instant coffee in water, containers for coffee paint, paint brushes, glue, pencil.

DIRECTIONS:
1. With a pencil, lightly sketch the outline of a picture on a tagboard background.
2. Rub glue in the areas where you want the coffee grounds to be a part of your picture. Sprinkle the coffee grounds on the glue and let the glue dry.
3. Complete your picture with "instant coffee paint."

EXTENSION: Write a story about your picture or write a description that explains how you made your picture.

WEAVING

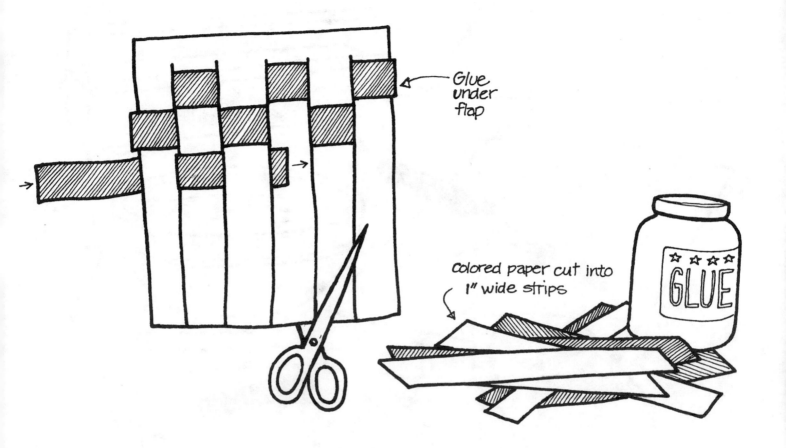

Glue under flap

colored paper cut into 1" wide strips

GLUE

MATERIALS: Various colors of construction paper, scissors, glue.

DIRECTIONS:
1. Cut slits in a sheet of paper to use as the base for the weaving project. (See the above illustration.)
2. Cut strips of paper for weaving in the base. Use different colors for the strips.
3. Weave the strips of paper in and out of the slits in the paper base. The first strip should begin on the top of the base and the second strip should begin on the bottom of the base. Continue to alternate the strips in this way.
4. Glue the ends of the strips to the paper base.

EXTENSION: Think of different uses for your weaving project and make a list of those uses.

WET CHALK DESIGNS

MATERIALS: Chalk sticks, paper, sponge, container of water, plastic cloth, waxed paper, apron or smock.

DIRECTIONS:
1. Put on an apron or smock.
2. Soak chalk in water for ten minutes.
3. Cover a table with a plastic cloth.
4. Making sure that your working space is properly protected, lay down a piece of paper and carefully apply water to it with a small sponge.
5. Make a design or a picture with the wet chalk.
6. Place your picture on a piece of waxed paper to dry.

EXTENSION: Write a story about your chalk picture.

ART RECIPES

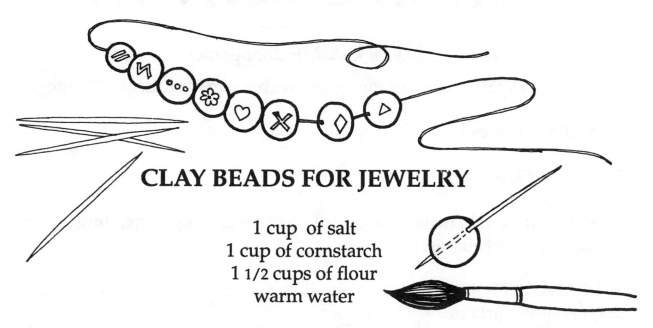

CLAY BEADS FOR JEWELRY

1 cup of salt
1 cup of cornstarch
1 1/2 cups of flour
warm water

Mix the dry ingredients. Add just enough warm water to make the clay workable. Roll the clay into balls about the size of marbles. Put a toothpick through the center of each of the balls of clay. When dry, paint and string the beads with elastic.

FINGER-PAINT PUDDING

1/2 cup of milk
1 tablespoon of dry pudding

Mix the milk and pudding in a plastic cup for three minutes. Then let the mixture set for five minutes. Spoon on paper and finger paint a picture. Let dry.

Tell a story about your picture.

Section 2 - GAMES

BINGO (indoor game)

OBJECTIVE: To fill all of the spaces with a marker to make "bingo."

AGES: All ages

PLAYERS: Any number

MATERIALS: Pencils, Bingo card on the following page, Bingo markers (buttons, paper squares, etc).

PREPARATION: Reproduce one Bingo card for each player. Give each player eight markers.

PREPARATION BY PLAYERS:
1. Without looking at anyone else's paper, each person writes the names of nine fruits on the lines of the nine Bingo boxes and draws a picture of each kind of fruit below the line in each box.
2. When all the players have completed their Bingo cards, the players, in turn, say one of the names of their fruits and the leader writes the names of these fruits on a sheet of paper to use for the bingo game. When each fruit is named, each player draws a dot in the corner of the square to show that this fruit has been mentioned. The next player says the name of a fruit that hasn't been said before. The preparation continues until every fruit that the players have written on the bingo card has been named aloud. After a player has a dot in each box, he/she says "pass" when it is his/her turn. When everyone passes, the fruits have all been named and the Bingo game can begin.

DIRECTIONS:
1. When the leader says the name of a fruit on the list, the players put a marker in their corresponding square, as in regular Bingo.
2. The player who fills his/her card first is the winner.

VARIATION: Use a variety of themes for this game (sports, animals, etc).

BINGO GAMECARD

_____	_____	_____
_____	_____	_____
_____	_____	_____

CONCENTRATE!
Indoor/Outdoor

OBJECTIVE: To remember where to go on a signal.

AGES: All ages

PLAYERS: 1 - 20

MATERIALS: Various colors of construction paper and a woodblock or a drum.

PREPARATION: Give each player a piece of colored construction paper.

DIRECTIONS:
1. Ask each player to stand in a designated area beside his/her piece of paper.
2. The leader hits the drum one time and explains that each time the drum is hit one time each player must stand beside his/her piece of paper.
3. Direct all players to leave the paper on the floor and then move beside a second piece of paper.
4. The leader hits the drum twice and explains that each player must stand beside the second piece of paper when two drum beats are heard.
5. Review several times: one drum beat and moving to the first piece of paper, and two drum beats and moving to the second piece of paper.
6. Hit the drum three times. Direct all players to move to a third piece of paper.
7. Play the game by changing the sequence of the beats.

VARIATIONS:
1. Add four and five places to move, using four and five drum beats.
2. Change the sounds. Use a drum for the first piece of paper, a triangle for the second piece of paper, a woodblock for the third piece of paper, and a tambourine for the fourth piece of paper, etc.

NOTE: This activity can be difficult for young children. Do not use more than three drum beats for young children and provide them with practice time. Older children will enjoy making this game complicated.

DETECTIVE
Indoor/Outdoor

OBJECTIVE: To identify a friend by listening to clues given by a leader.

AGES: All ages

PLAYERS: Any number

PREPARATION: Players are seated in a circle or on elevated steps or a hillside so that they are able to see each other.

DIRECTIONS:
1. The leader starts a simple clap pattern, such as "knees-hands-knees-hands." It is important to maintain a slow, steady tempo.
2. Everyone joins in the clap pattern which continues throughout the game.
3. The leader begins telling clues about one friend in the group. The group does not know who the leader is describing.
4. Six clues are chanted by the leader as everyone claps. These clues are echoed by the other players.
5. After four clues are given, the clapping stops and the players may raise their hands and guess the person.
6. If a player guesses correctly, he/she becomes the leader and the game begins again. If the player does not guess the right person, another player may guess. It might be necessary to start the clapping again and give another clue. This continues until someone guesses who the friend is.

EXAMPLE:
Leader begins a four-beat clap pattern and all join in.

LEADER:
I have a friend here. (Everyone echoes this sentence.)
She has long brown hair. (echo)
She is wearing jeans. (echo)
She has two sisters. (echo)
No tennis shoes today. (echo)
Can you guess who this is? (echo)

HOPSCOTCH SPELLING
Outdoor

OBJECTIVE: To spell the most words in a sentence.

AGES: 6 - 12

PLAYERS: Any number

MATERIALS: Stopwatch, paper for recording words, clipboard, pencil, chalk, and an outdoor cement area.

PREPARATION: Write a sentence such as , "It is fun to spell and play," on several lines with chalk on an outdoor cement area. Each sentence should contain the vowels, a, e, i, o, and u. The words on the hopscotch boards should be close enough together for easy jumping. Draw a square around each of the letters in this sentence as seen in the illustration below. Each team of two to four players will need one hopscotch board. The hopscotch boards should be a distance away from one another.

DIRECTIONS:
1. The first player from team #1 hops from one letter to another in order to spell one new word. The word is recorded on paper. The first player from team #2 hops from one letter to another to spell a new word. This is also recorded. This sequence is continued until all the players have had a turn.
2. The game is over when the leader, after a predetermined time says, "Stop." A stopwatch may be used.
3. With the leader's help, each team adds the total number of words that are spelled correctly. The team(s) with the most words wins the game.
4. The top winners write the next sentence on the hopscotch boards.

Words children can hop out from this example:
top
funny
spill
etc.

NUMBER HUNT
Indoor/Outdoor

OBJECTIVE: To get the highest total on math cards.

AGES: All ages

PLAYERS: Any number

MATERIALS: Black marker or crayon and 3" x 5" index cards or tagboard cut into 3" x 5" cards.

PREPARATION: Write a different numeral on each card. Use appropriate numbers for the age of the children who are playing the game.

DIRECTIONS:
1. The leader of the game hides each of the cards, leaving a small part of the card in view.
2. When the leader says "start," each player tries to find as many cards as possible.
3. When all the cards have been found, the leader says "stop."
4. Each player adds up the numerals on the cards that have been found. The player(s) with the highest total wins the game. The winner(s) gets to hide the cards when the game is played again.

RELAY RACES
Indoor/Outdoor

OBJECTIVE: To complete the relay faster than the opposing team.

AGES: All ages

PLAYERS: Any number

MATERIALS: Paper plates

PREPARATION: Make two chalk lines on the floor or sidewalk 12' - 14' apart. One line is the starting line and the other line is the turn-around line.

DIRECTIONS:
1. The leader numbers the children off by 1,2,1,2 count.
2. The players form two lines — ones and twos.
3. The first players on each team put the paper plates on top of their heads. When the leader says "start," the players walk from the starting line to the turn-around line and back, balancing the plates on their heads without touching them. They then give the plates to the next players. If the plate falls, the player returns to the starting line to try again.
4. The first team with all players to walk to the turn-around line and back again wins the game.

VARIATION: Equal numbers of objects may be put on each of the paper plates, such as lima beans, paper clips, and macaroni. If the plate and objects are dropped, they may be picked up, but the player must start over again.

SOME OTHER RELAY RACES
Indoor/Outdoor

• Carrying a feather on a spoon.

• Passing a rubber jar ring down the line on popsicle sticks which each player is holding.

• Giving each player a straw and napkin and having the players carry the paper napkin up and back by sucking on the straw.

• Moving a bucket of sand by having each player carry the sand one spoonful at a time from a full bucket to an empty bucket some distance away.

• Carrying a beanbag on the head while tossing another beanbag from hand to hand. If either bag is dropped, the player must start again.

TARGET MATH
Outdoor

OBJECTIVE: To get the highest math score.

AGES: All ages

PLAYERS: Any number

MATERIALS: Sidewalk or cement area, chalk, beanbags.

PREPARATION: Draw a target with chalk on the sidewalk with various numbers in each section of it, similar to the one in the illustration below.

DIRECTIONS:
1. Players take turns standing at the tossing line and tossing a bean bag onto the target, attempting to toss it into the section with the highest number.
2. After each turn, the total number of points are recorded and added up.
3. After each player has had three turns (or another specified number of turns), each player adds up his/her total score. The player with the highest total wins the game.

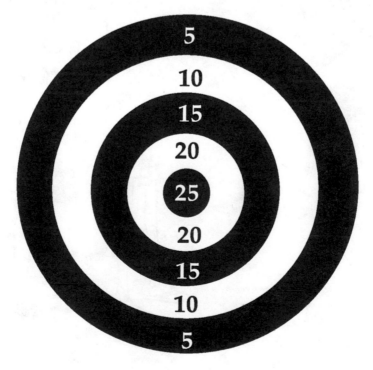

Section 3 - DRAMA

PANTOMIME

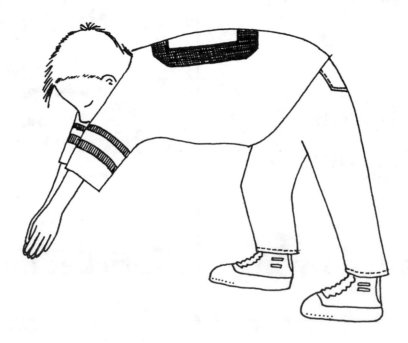

MATERIALS: Pantomime cards (found on pages 22 & 23) and a container to keep the cards in.

PREPARATION: Reproduce the pantomime cards. Cut out the cards and place them in the container. (Laminate for durability.)

DIRECTIONS:
1. The teacher reads the following definition: "Pantomime is using gestures and movement, without words or sounds, to convey an action, thought, or feeling." The class will pantomime actions.
2. The first player selects a card from the container, reads it silently, and pantomimes the action. The group has three chances to guess the correct action. The game continues until everyone has had a turn.

EXTENSION: Create and make your own pantomime cards using 3" x 5" index cards or paper cut into 3" x 5" strips.

Pantomime Cards

Pantomime each card by pretending that you are . . .

blowing up a balloon	gelatin on a plate
bacon in a frying pan	a chicken hatching
a plant growing	a cricket jumping
fishing	a worm wiggling on the ground
cutting grass with a push lawn mower	preparing potatoes for baking
kneading bread	cleaning up a broken egg

Pantomime Cards

Copy and cut-out.

Pantomime each card by pretending that you are . . .

getting ready for school	washing windows
washing dishes by hand	playing volleyball
putting clean sheets on a bed	making cookies
exploring the moon	watering house plants
buying groceries	eating spaghetti
washing your hair	folding laundry

PLAY STARTERS AND PUPPETS

Write a creative play, skit, or pantomime using your own title or one of the titles below:

IF ONLY I COULD SWIM
BEHIND THE BLUE DOOR
WHISTLE IF YOU NEED ME
NOW I KNOW HOW TO . . .
IT HAPPENED YESTERDAY
RACE TO THE FUTURE

PUPPETS

1. Make a sack puppet of an imaginary animal. Demonstrate the sound this animal would make.

2. Make finger puppets from removable paper such as Post-It-Tape or Post-It-Notes. Write a play for two to five characters. After you have practiced your play, present it to your friends or family.

3. Make stick puppets using tongue depressors. Write a play for your puppets.

4. Create your own puppets from throw-aways (bags, boxes, egg cartons, milk cartons, etc).

GRACEY'S MOTHER - a play

ACTRESSES AND ACTORS

NARRATOR   MS. SNIDER (Teacher)   KYLE
JERRY (Classmate)   JANE (Classmate)   PAM (Kyle's Sister)

NARRATOR: Kyle and Pam, his younger sister, are walking to school.

PAM: What kinds of eggs do you have in your classroom?

KYLE: We have chicken eggs from the hatchery and a goose egg from John's farm.

PAM: How long have you had them?

KYLE: More than two weeks. Our teacher says that it is nearly time for them to hatch.

PAM: I hope our class gets to see the babies after they hatch.

KYLE: I'm really EXCITED to see them too.

NARRATOR: Jerry, a classmate, joins Kyle.

JERRY: Hurry, Kyle! Let's go see if any of the eggs have hatched.

KYLE: Bye, Pam. I'll see you after school.

NARRATOR: As Kyle and Jerry enter their classroom, they join a group of children sitting around the table in the science center.

MS. SNIDER: As soon as you take your seats, I'll explain how all of you will have a chance to watch the eggs this morning.

NARRATOR: The children go to their seats.

MS. SNIDER: This is the day the eggs should hatch. Every ten minutes someone needs to check the eggs to tell the rest of us if there is any action. Here is a list of all your names. You might see a crack or hole in the egg or a tiny beak will appear. If you see a sign of hatching, please tell me so that we can watch it. It's important that you don't touch the eggs. Jane, your name is first on the list. In ten minutes, you go and check the eggs. The rest of you may begin silent reading.

NARRATOR: Everyone begins to read. After ten minutes Jane checks the eggs, then returns to her seat. After another ten minutes Jerry checks the eggs. The morning passes.

MS. SNIDER: It's time for lunch. Kyle, after you have eaten, check the eggs. Jerry, you can check the eggs at about 12:30. If any eggs hatch, please record the time on the chart.

NARRATOR: Everyone goes out the door for lunch.

NARRATOR: Ten minutes later Kyle comes into the classroom and observes the eggs. He hurries to his desk to get a pencil, looks at the clock, and records the time on the chart. He watches intently, and again, writes on the chart.

KYLE: Oh no, so many are hatching all at once! I wish someone else were here to help me with the chart.

NARRATOR: Kyle goes to the chart to record more information. Jerry enters the classroom.

KYLE: Oh Jerry, I'm glad you're here. So many of the eggs are hatching and I can't record and observe at the same time. The big egg hatched at 12:25. Isn't that baby cute?

JERRY: Wow, look at all those babies! Look at the big one walking toward you. It must like you Kyle.

KYLE: I hope we get to hold the babies today.

JERRY: Oh look, there's another chick coming out of its egg. I'll record this one.

NARRATOR: As the children come back into the classroom, they all gather with excitement around the babies in the cage.

MS. SNIDER: *(to the class)* Come and sit in a circle on the floor. I'll put the cage in the middle of the circle and we'll all watch to see what the chicks do when I let them out.

NARRATOR: Children move from their seats and sit in a circle as Ms. Snider carefully carries the cage to the center of the circle and opens the door.

MS. SNIDER: Kyle, please go get the chart so we can also record what the babies are doing now.

NARRATOR: Kyle gets the chart, sits down, carefully picks up the gosling and gently pets it. The gosling makes soft sounds.

MS. SNIDER: Kyle, since the gosling seems to like you so much, why don't you select a name for it while the rest of us think of names for the chicks.

NARRATOR: The children brainstorm names for the chicks as Kyle admires the gosling in his hand.

KYLE: Ms. Snider, I think I'd like to name the gosling "Gracey."

JANE: I think Gracey the goose thinks Kyle is her mother.

(Everyone laughs.)

MS. SNIDER: Let's put the babies back in the cage so we can do a rap for Gracey.

NARRATOR: Everyone collects the babies, puts them in cages and forms a ring around Ms. Snider.

MS. SNIDER: We're ready to do a rap for Gracey. Be my echo. *(Ms. Snider stands and starts a slow four-beat snap and leads the rap.)*

MS. SNIDER	EVERYONE
Gracey, the goose	Echo
When she gets loose	Echo
She follows Kyle	Echo
She likes his style	Echo
Gracey, the goose	Echo
Yes, Gracey, the goose.	Echo

SANDRA'S DISCOVERY - a play

ACTRESSES AND ACTORS

NARRATOR	AUNT DEE
SANDRA DEE JONES	SANDRA'S MOTHER
TRACEY (Sandra's Friend)	SANDRA'S FATHER
BETH (Sandra's Best Friend)	JEFF (Sandra's Friend)
SAM (Sandra's Friend)	SALLY (Sandra's Friend)

NARRATOR: It's a beautiful sunny afternoon in Sandra's backyard. Sandra and her best friend, Beth, are talking and drinking apple juice at the picnic table.

BETH: Why the big frown, Sandra?

SANDRA: Mom and Dad are going to England for two weeks and they told me this morning that my Aunt Dee is coming to stay with me while they're on the trip.

BETH: Who's Aunt Dee?

SANDRA: She's my Mom's sister. I don't even know her. All I know is that my middle name "Dee" is the same as her first name. She has been working in Japan, Hong Kong, Australia, and other places. I don't remember if she ever came to see us before. I'll be staying with someone I don't even know.

BETH: Maybe she'll be fun.

SANDRA: I'll be bored for two whole weeks. I wish I could stay with you.

NARRATOR: A car door slams in front of the house.

MOTHER: Sandra, I have a surprise for you. Guess who came earlier than expected?

SANDRA: (whispering to Beth) Oh, she came early?

BETH: Maybe it's good she came early. This way you can get to know her before your parents leave. Besides, you can come to my house any time you want if you need to get away from your house.

(Mother and Aunt Dee enter. Aunt Dee is wearing leis around her neck.)

MOTHER: Dee, this is Sandra and her friend Beth. Sandra, come say "Hello" to your Aunt Dee.

SANDRA: *(She walks slowly toward Aunt Dee with her head down.)* "Hello." *(Returns to chair.)*

AUNT DEE: Aloha, Sandra. Aloha, Beth. *(Aunt Dee walks toward the girls and places a lei around the neck of each of them.)*

BETH: Wow! A real orchid lei. Thanks!

SANDRA: *(softly)* Thank you.

MOTHER: Aunt Dee brought a fresh pineapple from Hawaii, too. Let's see how it tastes.

NARRATOR: Everyone moves into the kitchen and sits around a table.

AUNT DEE: Let's have a pineapple party while your mother goes shopping. Do you know how to cut pineapple sticks? We can make orange juice and chocolate dips. You can invite a couple of friends to our party if you want.

NARRATOR: It is thirty minutes later near the picnic table. Sandra has just finished introducing her friends, Sally, Sam, Tracey, and Jeff, to Aunt Dee.

(Everyone pantomimes eating and dipping pineapple sticks.)

AUNT DEE: Please say your names one more time.

SALLY: I'm Sally, and this is my brother, Sam.

TRACEY: My name is Tracey and this is my brother, Jeff.

AUNT DEE: Hello, everyone. My name is Dee. Welcome to our pineapple party. After we eat, we'll pick daisies and I'll show you how to make a Hawaiian lei with them.

SAM: Do you live in Hawaii?

AUNT DEE: No, but I do a lot of traveling for my work and I stopped in Hawaii on my way to visit Sandra.

SALLY: Can you hula?

AUNT DEE: I know a few movements. This means "water" *(wave hands up and down to imitate waves)* and this means "come here." *(With palms up, make beckoning gesture towards you.)*

BETH: Sandra, it looks like you are going to have fun next week.

AUNT DEE: Oh, we're all going to have fun.

SANDRA: *(whispering to Beth)* Maybe staying with Aunt Dee isn't going to be so bad after all.

NARRATOR: Two weeks later Sandra's mother and father return from their trip.

SANDRA: *(Sandra hugs her mom and dad.)* Hi, I'm glad to see you. Did you have fun? Was the plane neat? Did you see the Changing of the Guards in England?

FATHER: *(laughing)* Slow down, Sandra. We'll tell you all about it right after I put the suitcases in the bedroom.

MOTHER: You two look like you've been busy making paper projects.

SANDRA: Oh, yes, Mom. Aunt Dee showed me how to make origami, and Chinese kites, and to do the hula, and we even cooked Japanese tempura.

FATHER: Well, Sandra Dee, it sounds like you had a good time while we were away.

SANDRA: I did. Aunt Dee is really fun. I'm glad that you named me after her.

AUNT DEE: I'm glad they did too. *(Aunt Dee and Sandra hug each other.)*

SANDRA'S DISCOVERY - Activities

1. Make leis from tissue paper and string.

2. Make origami items from paper.

3. Clean and taste a fresh pineapple.

ZACH'S SURPRISE - a play

ACTRESSES AND ACTORS

NARRATOR	KENDRA (Classmate)
ZACH	JACK (Classmate)
TONY (Zach's New Friend)	JOE (Classmate)
MR. BRIGHT (Teacher)	AMY (Classmate)

NARRATOR: Tony and Zach are talking while they walk to school.

TONY: Zach, I'm glad you moved next door. Now we both have someone to walk to school with every day.

ZACH: Me too. It's neat to make a friend right away when you've just moved to a new place.

TONY: I tried to call you last night to see if you wanted to play soccer, but your dad said that you were at a lesson.

ZACH: Yeah, I was at my ballet lesson.

TONY: *(surprised)* Ballet? I didn't know boys took ballet lessons!

ZACH: Sure, boys take ballet lessons. It's really fun and good exercise too.

TONY: Well, you better not tell the other kids you're taking ballet lessons. They might make fun of you.

NARRATOR: Tony and Zach hurry into their classroom. The bell rings and they sit down at their desks.

MR. BRIGHT: Let's start the day by having each person tell about an activity that they like to do. This might be something at school or home or someplace else. Let's start with Kendra.

KENDRA: I like to play the piano. I take piano lessons every week and it is really fun.

JACK: My Dad and I build model airplanes together. It takes a lot of time and patience, but it's worth it.

JOE: I like to play baseball.

AMY: I collect stamps as a hobby and I put them in stamp books. I have stamps from forty-three countries.

(Optional: other children in the class name their favorite thing to do.)

TONY: I like to play soccer. It's great fun!

ZACH: I like to play soccer, too, I guess.

(Tony gives Zach a puzzled look.)

MR. BRIGHT: It has been interesting to hear all about the different things that you like to do. I'd like to know more about each of your interests, so for our writing assignment today, you may write about your favorite thing to do.

NARRATOR: Everyone begins to write, except Zach. He sits staring at the paper in front of him.

TONY: *(whispering)* What's the matter Zach, can't you get going?

NARRATOR: Zach shrugs.

MR. BRIGHT: *(walks toward Zach)* Zach, do you need some help?

ZACH: *(softly)* I . . . I . . . really can't write about soccer because I don't know anything about it.

MR. BRIGHT: Then why did you say you like soccer?

ZACH: (*embarrassed*) I . . . I . . . only said that soccer was what I like to do because that's what Tony said. I was afraid to say that I liked ballet best because I didn't want anyone to laugh at me.

MR. BRIGHT: Ballet! How wonderful! I took ballet in college and loved it. In fact, the football team warmed up with ballet exercises every day. That's how I got interested in it.

NARRATOR: The next day in school after Kendra, Amy, and Jack read their writing assignments, Mr. Bright calls on Zach.

MR. BRIGHT: We've really had some interesting reports. Zach, it's your turn to share what you and I **BOTH** like to do.

NARRATOR: Zach jumps up with a big smile.

ZACH: I know that I said that I like soccer but what I really like is ballet. I'm going to start my report with showing you two ballet steps.

NARRATOR: Everyone looks surprised! Zach demonstrates the ballet steps and the class applauds enthusiastically.

ZACH'S SURPRISE - Activities

1. Research the five ballet feet positions. Use an encyclopedia or a reference book about ballet.

2. Draw and label the five ballet feet positions on a piece of paper. Can you perform these five positions?

3. Name several famous ballets.

Section 4 - MUSIC and MOVEMENT

ALPHABET RAP GAME

AGES: 8 - 12

PLAYERS: Any number

MATERIALS: 3" x 5" index cards

PREPARATION: Make alphabet cards — one letter on each card. Make category cards, one category on each card. (See category list on page 37.)

DIRECTIONS:
1. Divide your class into two teams.
2. Each team selects someone to record their words. Each team selects one player to choose a card.
3. Start a slow "snap rap." Snap the fingers in 1-2-3-4 time and teach the rap on the next page. (X's indicate where the snaps occur in the rap.)
4. Say the rap. A player from team 1 selects a card from the alphabet card pile. A player from team 2 selects a card from the category card pile.
5. On the word GO the teams begin to make a list of all the words in the category beginning with the alphabet letter selected.
6. The length of the game is predetermined by the teacher. Both teams must stop when the teacher says "Stop." The team with the most correct words for that category wins.

> EXAMPLE:
> Team 1 selects the card with letter B.
> Team 2 selects the category "fruit."
>
> Each team makes a list of fruits that begin with the letter B.
> banana   blueberry   blackberry
> boysenberry black raspberry

AN ALPHABET RAP

Snap fingers where the 'x' is located on the rap. There are four snaps on each line.

```
  x           x              x     x
Twenty-six letters in the alphabet
  x           x        x         x
Twenty-six letters we can name
  x       x              x            x
Pull one letter from the pile right here
  x       x          x         x
And you play the alphabet game.


  x           x              x     x
Take one card  from the other pile
  x           x        x         x
This is the category we must know
  x       x        x       x
Everyone ready, get set now
  x       x        x       x
Come on team, and let's go.
```

CATEGORY SUGGESTIONS:

Names	Flowers	Furniture	Fruit	Tools
States	Careers	Clothing	Animals	Toys

(Create category cards using your own ideas.)

BUBBLE BLOWING CHAMP

All: Ready - Set - Go
All: 1-2-3-4-5-6-7-8-9-10.

Choose two players to chew bubble gum and blow bubbles.
The person with the largest bubble stands out of the circle.
Repeat the game five times.
Have the five finalists line up.
All count to twenty as the five finalists blow bubbles.
Have a daily contest. Continue for a week and have a "Bubble Blowing Weekly
    Champ."

WE'RE GOING FISHING

AGES: All ages

The leader says each line while performing the action indicated in the parentheses. The participants echo and repeat the actions.

WE'RE GOING FISHING

We're going fishing *(pat each knee in walking beat)* — echo

Down at the pond *(move hand in a waving motion)* — echo

The frogs are hopping *(clap hands sharply)* — echo

The fish are jumping *(snap fingers)* — echo

The bugs are biting *(wave hands as if shooing away bugs)* — echo

The cattails are swaying *(sway back and forth)* — echo

Pick out some bait *(pantomime)* — echo

Put it on a hook *(pantomime)* — echo

Throw out the line *(pantomime)* — echo

Hold the pole tightly *(pantomime)* — echo

Wait for a jerk *(large upward motion and jerk)* — echo

WOW! I caught a fish *(admire fish)* — echo

Take it off the hook *(pantomime)* — echo

Return it to the water *(pantomime)* — echo

Pack up your gear *(pantomime)* — echo

Time to go home *(pat knees in walking beat)* — echo

Swat the mosquitoes *(swat arms in steady beat)* — echo

Wave at your friends *(wave)* — echo

Now say good-bye *(frame mouth with hands)* — echo

JUMP ROPE CHANTS

The following chants are to be chanted as players jump.

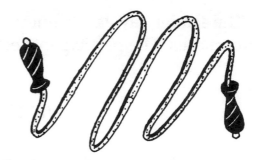

WATERMELON
Watermelon, watermelon, summer treat.
How many slices can you eat?
1-2-3-4-5, etc.

PENNIES
I dropped in my pennies and they went CLANK!
How many pennies are in my piggy bank?
1-2-3-4-5, etc.

JUMP
Jump, jump, jump so high.
How many jumps 'til I reach the sky?
1-2-3-4-5, etc.

CROAKING FROGS
Croaking, croaking, croaking frogs.
How many sitting on those logs?
1-2-3-4-5, etc.

LIGHTNING BUG
Lightning bug, lightning bug, tiny spark.
Count each one you see in the dark.
1-2-3-4-5, etc.

STARS
Blinking, blinking, blinking light.
How many stars in the sky at night?
1-2-3-4-5, etc.

JUMP ROPE CHANTS TO SING

BETTY JEAN

Bet - ty Jean, dressed in green. Went to the kit-chen to

eat a sar - dine There she ate a bug in - stead

How man - y days did she stay in bed.

PICNIC TIME
Barbeque fun, hamburger bun.
Have a picnic in the sun.
Flies arrive and want to stay.
How many flies did you shoo away?
1-2-3-4-5, etc.

BEN
Ben, Ben, tall and lean.
He flew right off in a magic machine.
Flew right over the moon they say.
How many days did he stay away?
1-2-3-4-5, etc.

MOTIONS AND MEMORY

DORIS DUCK
Make motions as you say the verse.

Doris Duck *(bend knees and put hands on knees)*
Goes quack, quack, quack *(make hands into duck mouth)*
She wobbles in the front *(wobble head and shoulder)*
She wobbles in the back *(wobble hips and legs)*
She steps to the left *(one step to the left)*
She steps to the right *(one step to the right)*
She tries to jump *(make a very small jump)*
But just can't quite!

After the poem has been learned, repeat the entire poem seven times, leaving out one line each time, but doing the actions. The last time only the last line will be spoken.

Draw a picture of Doris Duck in the box below. Is she wearing a hat? Is she near a pond?

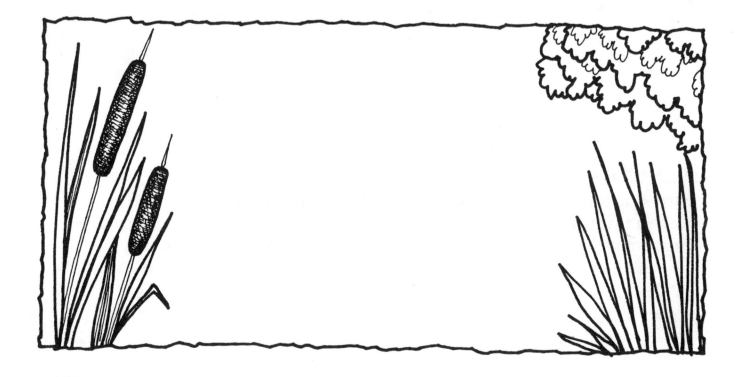

MOTIONS AND MEMORY

LUCY LADYBUG

Make the motions as you say the verse.

Lucy Ladybug likes to fly *(bend arms to look like wings)*
She spreads her wings and goes up high *(make flying motions with arms)*
Wings at her side, now down to the ground *(bend near the ground)*
She hops on a rose and looks all around. *(hop and look around)*

Draw a picture of Lucy. Remember she has spots on her back.

POPCORN MACHINE

POPCORN MACHINE -Activity

MATERIALS: Throw-aways such as boxes, paper tubes, plastic bottles, milk cartons, pieces of wood, scraps of tile or linoleum.

After you have learned the song, "Popcorn Machine," create your own machine from "junk." Build this machine from discarded materials. What is the name of your machine? What is its purpose? Make an illustration of your machine in the box below.

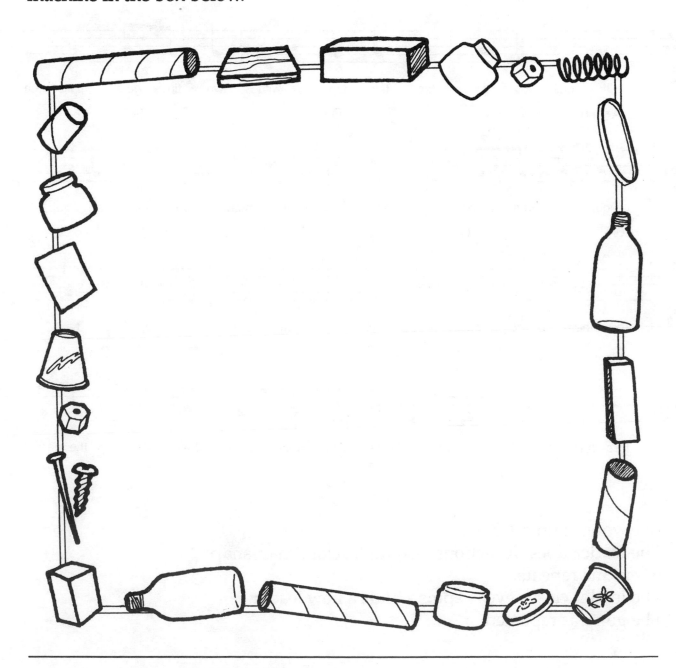

SNAP, CLAP, TAP, RAP

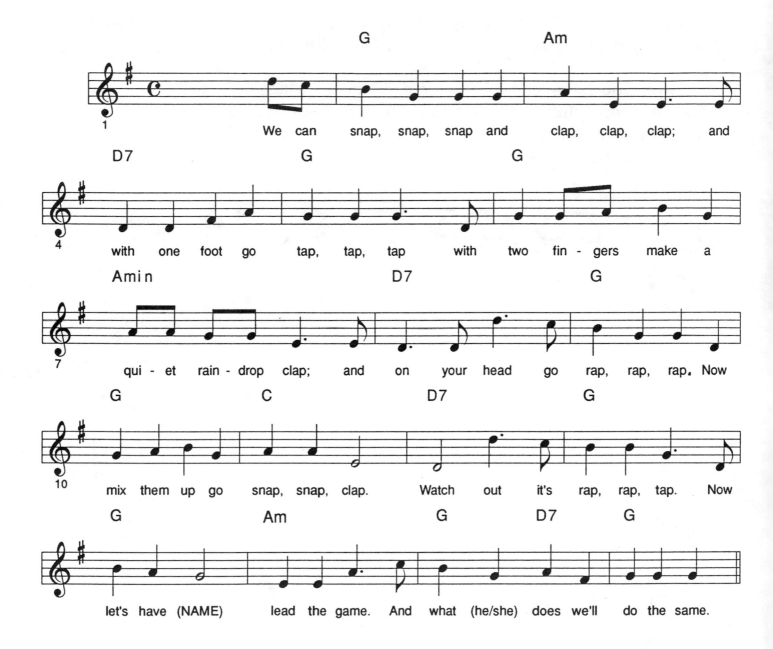

Everyone counts 1-2-3-4.

The leader does the actions - example: clap, snap-snap.

Everyone repeats.

The leader closes eyes - spins - finds a new leader.

The game is repeated.

WIGGLE - GIGGLE FUN

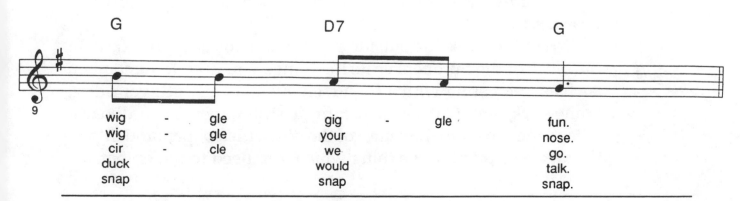

Section 5 - HODGEPODGE

FUN WITH BOXES

CAR OF THE FUTURE

Materials: Box, scissors, glue, crayons or markers, scrap fabric, glitter, sequins or anything else you may have available to decorate your car of the future.

Directions: Using a box as the body of the car, design a car of the future. You may cut away parts of the box, glue other items to the box, or color features on the box. Hold an "unveiling" for friends, family, or classmates and explain your project.

NEW TELEVISION PROGRAM

Materials: Box, crayons or colored pencils, magazines, scissors, glue.

Directions: Write a story or script for a new television program. Make a scene for the new program by drawing and/or gluing pictures from old magazines in the inside bottom of the box. Stand the box on its side to resemble a television screen. Tell the story of your new program to a friend. Write more stories for the program together.

REMINDER CLOCK

Materials: Box, crayons, pencil or pen, stiff paper or cardboard, scissors, brad.

Directions: Use the outside bottom of a box as a clock face. In the place of the numbers write the things you need to remember, such as a meeting with a friend, chores, a walk with your dog, homework, etc. Cut an arrow from stiff paper or cardboard. Attach the arrow to the center of the box with a paper brad. Move the arrow to point to the thing which you need to remember.

FUN WITH COTTON BALLS

COTTON BALL ART
Materials: Cotton balls, paper, crayons.
Directions: Make a list of ways that you could use a cotton ball in a picture. A cotton ball, for example, could be used for a cloud. Then draw a picture including one to three cotton balls as part of the picture.

CREATIVE WRITING
Materials: Cotton balls, paper, pencil.
Directions: Write a story by using your own "story starter" or one of the "story starters" below:
      1. One day a cotton ball fell on my head.
          It was so light that...
      2. "Let me out! Let me out!"
          yelled a soft, white cotton ball.

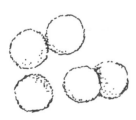

COTTON BALL GAME
Materials: Cotton balls, paper, pencil, recyclable items such as paper bowls, paper cups, paper tubes, and egg cartons.
Directions: Create a game with the cotton balls. Write directions for the game on a sheet of paper. Then demonstrate the game. Have fun!

BOX SHOW
Materials: Pencil; long strips of paper such as adding machine tape; milk carton.
What you do: Read as much as possible about how cotton is grown. Draw pictures on a long sheet of paper to slide through a box. Make a display box, as seen in the illustration, to slide pictures through so that you can show others how cotton is grown.

FUN WITH CRAFT STICKS

CRAFT STICK ART

Materials: Craft sticks, heavy paper or cardboard, crayons or colored pencils, glue.

Directions: Sketch two or more ways that you could use craft sticks in a picture. Then choose your favorite sketch to use as an idea for your picture. Draw your picture and glue the craft sticks in place.

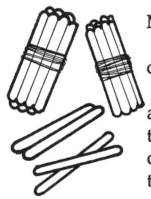

MATH STORIES

Materials: Craft sticks, rubber bands, paper, pencils, index cards.

Directions: Put a rubber band around ten craft sticks to make a set. Make several sets of ten sticks and also leave separate sticks to use as ones. Write math stories on a sheet of paper using the sets of tens and the individual sticks as counters. Write the answer on the back of an index card and ask an adult to check to see that it is correct. Ask others to read and write the answers to your math stories.

CRAFT BOX

Materials: Craft sticks, glue, paper.

Directions: Use craft sticks to make a wooden box for holding note cards or coasters. Glue the craft sticks together as seen in the illustration. Cut paper into note-size pieces or into coasters.

PUPPETS

Materials: Craft sticks, scraps of paper, scissors, glue, paper, pencil.

Directions: Design paper puppets and glue them on craft sticks. Write a puppet play. Perform your play.

FUN WITH ENVELOPES

HAND PUPPET

Materials: Envelopes slightly wider than your hand, scissors, crayons or colored pencils.

Directions: Cut two holes, (the size of your fingers) equally spaced, in the bottom edge of the envelope. Hold the envelope upside down with the flap hanging down. Using the flap as a beak, nose or chin, draw a person's or animal's face on the front of the envelope. Insert your fingers in the holes as ears and make up a play for your hand puppet.

MESSAGE HOLDER

Materials: Envelope, string or yarn, scissors or hole punch, crayons or markers, paper and pencil.

Directions: Punch or cut a hole at the top of both sides of the envelope just below the flap. Tie one end of a 12" piece of string or yarn through each hole. Decorate the front of the envelope. Use the envelope as a message holder and hang it on a doorknob or drawer handle to leave notes for friends and family.

ENVELOPE TOWN

Materials: Envelopes of varying sizes, crayons or colored pencils.

Directions: Each envelope, with the flap as the roof, will be a different house or building in a town. Decorate the front of the envelopes with doors, windows, bushes, curtains, etc. Build a town with your friends or classmates. Lay your town out on the floor with spaces for streets between the buildings. You can also moisten the glue on the envelope flap and then stick the envelopes to a large sheet of butcher paper. Hang the butcher paper on a wall to display your town.

FUN WITH INDEX CARDS

NAME CARD

Materials: Index card, crayons or colored pencils, scissors.

Directions: Fold an index card in half lengthwise so it will stand like a tent. Write a name and draw decorations on the side. Stand it up to use as a name card on a table or desk.

DESCRIPTION CARD

Materials: Index card, crayons or colored pencils.

Directions: On one side of an index card write a description or definition of something. On the other side of the card draw a picture of it. You can make a whole set of cards for fun with friends and family.

PICTURE OR PHOTO FRAME

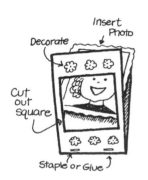

Materials: Two index cards, a picture or photo the same size or smaller than the index cards, crayons or colored pencils, stapler or tape.

Directions: Cut a square out of the center of one of the index cards. Lay this card on top of the other one and staple or tape the two together down the sides and across the bottom, leaving the top open. Decorate around the hole in the front card. Slide in your picture or photo so it can be seen through the hole.

GREETING CARDS

Materials: Index cards, crayons or colored pencils.

Directions: Fold an index card in half from the left side to the right side. Decorate the blank front side of the card. You can make birthday cards, get-well cards and many other kinds of cards.

NAPKIN RINGS

Materials: Index cards, pencil or pen, ruler, crayons or colored pencils, glue, scissors, napkin.

Directions: Cut a card lengthwise into 1" strips. Decorate each strip and glue the ends together to form a ring. Roll the napkin and slide through.

FUN WITH LIDS

LID ART

Materials: Various sizes of lids, colored construction paper, pencil.

Directions: With a pencil, trace around the lids on construction paper. Cut out the shapes and glue them on a piece of paper to make a design or picture.

PUZZLE

Materials: Plastic or cardboard lid, crayons, scissors.

Directions: Cut out the flat, round part of a lid leaving the rim as the frame for a puzzle. Make a picture on the flat, round part of the lid. Then cut it into pieces to make a puzzle which can be reassembled inside the frame.

LID SPIRAL

Materials: Lid, pencil, scissors, paper, glue, paper clip, string.

Directions: Trace around a large lid on a sheet of construction paper. Cut out the circle and then cut it to make a spiral as seen in the illustration. Cut out and glue small construction paper designs on the spiral and decorate it. Punch a very small hole in the top of the spiral with the end of a paper clip. Make a knot on one end of a piece of string and thread the other end through the hole in the top of the spiral. Tie a paper clip on the other end of the string to use as a hanger. Hang your spiral in a special place.

MEASUREMENT

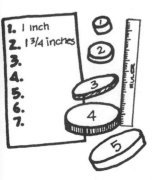

Materials: Various sizes of circular lids that are numbered from 1 to 10, paper, pencil, ruler.

Directions: Write the numerals from 1 to 10 on a sheet of paper. Measure the various sizes of lids to find the diameter of each of them. Write the measurements of each lid next to the appropriate numeral.

FUN WITH MAGAZINES

WORD SCRAMBLE
Materials: Magazines, scissors, box.

Directions: Cut individual words from old magazines. Place the words in a box. With friends, family, or classmates, take turns drawing ten words from the box and then laying them on a table to form a sentence.

TREASURE BOX
Materials: Cardboard box, magazines, glue, scissors.

Directions: Cover a cardboard box, such as an oatmeal box or a bakery box with a variety of pictures cut out of old magazines, gluing the pictures to the sides and top of the box. Use the box to store treasured items such as letters, sport cards, toys, etc.

STORY BOOK
Materials: Magazines, scissors, glue, paper, pencil or pen.

Directions: From an old magazine, cut out some pictures. Write a story, poem, or play about the pictures and glue them to the pages of your story for illustrations.

NUMBER GAME
Materials: Magazines, paper, scissors, pencil or pen.

Directions: Cut out numbers from old magazines. Glue them to small slips of paper. On separate pieces of paper write the symbols for addition(+), subtraction(-), multiplication (x), and division (÷). Using the slips of paper with numerals and the pieces of paper with mathematical symbols, arrange math problems and then solve them. You can challenge friends or classmates to solve the problems you set up.

FUN WITH PAPER TUBES

PICTURE FRAME

Materials: Two toilet paper tubes, one half-sheet of white tagboard for a picture, crayons, magazine pages for covering tubes, scissors.

Directions: Decorate the tubes by gluing pages of magazines around two toilet paper tubes. Cut a slot from the top of the tubes to one half inch from the bottom. Draw a picture on a sheet of paper. Then slide the sides of the paper into the slots of the tubes to make the picture stand up.

TUBE PUPPETS

Materials: Long paper towel tubes, colored markers or crayons, scraps of colored construction paper, pieces of yarn, scissors, glue, pencil, paper.

Directions: Color a person, animal, or object at the top of each tube to make a tube puppet. The bottom of the tube can be used as a handle. Write a play by yourself or with a friend for your new puppets. Kneel behind a table or desk, holding the puppets at tabletop level. You may move a puppet up and down or back and forth when it is speaking. Perform your play for your friends and family.

RING GAME

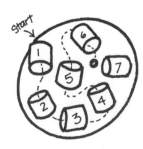

Materials: Paper tubes cut into half-inch rings, scissors, bead or marble, sturdy paper plate, marker, glue.

Directions: Glue the sides of the rings on a paper plate in a random pattern. Write a numeral on each of the rings in the order that you want a bead or marble to roll through each of them. The object of the game is to roll a bead through each of the rings in the correct order. Play your ring game with a friend.

FUN WITH STRAWS

STRAW PAINTING

Materials: Paints, paint containers, straws, paper.

Directions: Put a small amount of paint on a piece of paper. Carefully blow the paint around the paper to create a design.

STRAW AND CLAY

Materials: Straw, clay, scissors.

Directions: Create some three-dimensional objects from old straws and clay. You might, for example, design a merry-go-round with straws and clay.

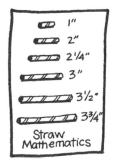

STRAW FLOWERS

Materials: Straws, scissors, facial tissues, scraps of green construction paper.

Directions: Pinch the center of a facial tissue, and pull up the sides of the tissue to resemble a flower blossom. Stick it into one end of a straw that will represent the stem. Cut out and glue construction paper leaves on the straw. You might put your flower in a vase or give it as a gift to a relative or friend.

STRAW MATHEMATICS

Materials: Straws, pencil, paper, ruler, glue, piece of cardboard.

Directions: Cut straws for the following lengths: 1 inch, 2 inches, 2 1/2 inches, 3 inches, 3 1/2 inches and 3 3/4 inches. Glue each of them on a piece of cardboard and record the length of each of them.

FUN WITH STRING AND YARN

SPIDER WEB.

Materials: String or yarn, paper, glue.

Directions: Read about spiders and their webs. On a piece of paper, glue string or yarn in the shape of a web. Are all spider webs shaped the same way? Write a story or poem about a spider and its web. Read it to family, friends, or classmates and show them your web.

YARN HAT

Materials: Yarn, box or paper bag, glue, (optional: odds and ends).

Directions: Find a box or paper bag which will fit your head like a hat. Glue different colored yarns and other odds and ends, such a feathers, sequins, buttons, or colored pieces of paper, to the box or bag. Model your hat for your friends and family.

STRING AND YARN PICTURE

Materials: String, yarn, paper glue, crayons or colored pencils, pencil or pen.

Directions: Create a picture by gluing different pieces of string and different colors of yarn on a sheet of paper. You may make grass, trees, outlines of houses, etc. Label your picture with a title and sign your name by gluing string or yarn in the shape of the letters in your name.

KEY CHAIN HANGER

Materials: Different colored yarns, scissors.

Directions: Make a 7" braid using several different colors of yarn. Thread a key on the braided end and knot the two ends of the braid together. These braids may be colored coded for keys.

Section 6 - NUTRITIOUS SNACKS

RECIPE CARDS
Cut out each recipe card and use it when you make a snack.

PERKY PRETZELS

INGREDIENTS: Pretzel sticks, tomatoes, strawberries, pineapple chunks, grapes, orange slices, cheese chunks, and other foods that can be slipped onto pretzel sticks.

UTENSILS: Paper plates for the perky pretzels.

DIRECTIONS:
1. Put a piece of food on each pretzel stick.
2. Place these food sticks in an interesting arrangement on a plate.

YOGRAMS

INGREDIENTS: Graham crackers; strawberry, blueberry or raspberry yogurt; 1/2 banana.

UTENSILS: Plastic knife and spoon, paper plate for graham crackers, a small cup for yogurt.

DIRECTIONS:
1. Spread the yogurt on the graham cracker.
2. Slice bananas and put them on top of the yogurt -covered cracker.

RECIPE CARDS

Cut out each recipe card and use it when you make a snack.

CRUNCHY CREATIONS

INGREDIENTS: A variety of raw vegetables: peeled potatoes, cucumber slices, carrot strips, lettuce, onion slices, cherry tomatoes, zucchini slices, snow peas, slices of yellow squash, radishes, mushrooms.

UTENSILS: Paper plate and plastic knife.

DIRECTIONS:
1. Arrange the vegetables to create an imaginary animal, person, or object on your plate.
2. Give your creation a name.
3. "Show-and-tell" your creation before you eat it.

PRETTY PUDDING

INGREDIENTS: Instant pudding, (1 large box for 6 children), 1/2 banana, milk, blueberries (or other fruit).

UTENSILS: Transparent plastic glass, plastic spoon, plastic knife, paper or plastic cup for mixing pudding, bowl for fruit.

DIRECTIONS: (individual serving)
1. Mix 1/2 cup milk with 1 tablespoon of instant pudding until thickened.
2. Let pudding set until slightly thick, then spoon the pudding and fruit in layers into the transparent plastic glass.

RECIPE CARDS

Cut out each recipe card and use it when you make a snack.

POPCORN PLEASERS

INGREDIENTS: Popped corn; raisins; shelled, unsalted sunflower seeds; and low-sugar cereal.

UTENSILS: Small paper or plastic bowl, plastic spoon, measuring cups.

DIRECTIONS:
Put the following ingredients in a bowl and mix well.
1. 1/2 cup of popped corn
2. 1/3 cup raisins
3. 1/4 cup sunflower seeds
4. 1/2 cup of low-sugared cereal

SMILING SANDWICH

INGREDIENTS: Slice of bread and special ingredients for a face such as olives, pickles, small pieces of red pepper, raisins, carrots, celery, peanut butter.

UTENSILS: Plastic knife, cookie cutter that cuts a circle, waxed paper to put the bread on.

DIRECTIONS:
1. Use the cookie cutter to cut a circle from the slice of bread.
2. Frost the circle with peanut butter.
3. Make a face with the special ingredients.

RECIPE CARDS

Cut out each recipe card and use it when you make a snack.

APRICOT ADE

INGREDIENTS: Apricot nectar (juice), ice milk or ice cream.

UTENSILS: Paper or plastic cup, spoon, measuring cups (1/3 and 1/4 cups).

DIRECTIONS:
1. Put 1/4 cup of apricot nectar in a cup.
2. Add 1/3 cup of ice milk.
3. Stir until the ice milk has dissolved.

FRUIT KABOBS

INGREDIENTS: Various kinds of fruits such as melons, orange slices, strawberries, grapes, grapefruit slices, pineapple chunks, etc.; and 4 pieces of uncooked spaghetti or bamboo sticks for kabob sticks.

UTENSILS: Paper plate to hold fruit kabobs.

DIRECTIONS:
1. Cut the fruit into pieces.
2. Hold 4 pieces of spaghetti tightly together in a bunch as you push the fruits on to all four pieces of the spaghetti.
3. Place the fruit kabobs on a plate and serve.

Section 7 - SIDEWALK CAREERS

SIDEWALK ADVERTISER

I can be a "Sidewalk Advertiser"
when I create interesting advertisements on the sidewalk.

HOW TO BE A SIDEWALK ADVERTISER

MATERIALS: Sidewalk chalk, (clipboard, paper, and pencil are optional).

SIDEWALK FUN:

1. Create and draw an advertisement for a product. This product may be one that you have created yourself or it may be one that is currently on the market.

2. Make some sketches of various ideas for advertisements on paper before you draw one on the sidewalk.

3. After you have made plans for your advertisement, draw it on the sidewalk to advertise the product. Have fun!

4. Share your advertisement with others. Tell them where you got your idea for the advertisement and why you think that your advertisement could help sell the product.

SIDEWALK ARTIST

I can be a "Sidewalk Artist" when I create pictures or designs
on the sidewalk for people to enjoy as they pass by.

HOW TO BE A SIDEWALK ARTIST

MATERIALS: Colored sidewalk chalk.

SIDEWALK FUN:
1. Create and draw pictures or designs on the sidewalk.

2. Illustrate a familiar fairy tale on the sidewalk.

3. Write a poem and illustrate it on the sidewalk.

4. On the sidewalk, create a picture that you think would look good in your
   home or school.

SIDEWALK CARTOONIST

**I can be a "Sidewalk Cartoonist" when I create and draw
my own comic strip or cartoon on the sidewalk.**

HOW TO BE A SIDEWALK CARTOONIST

MATERIALS: Colored sidewalk chalk, cartoons and comic strips from newspapers, paper, pencil.

SIDEWALK FUN:
1. Read a number of cartoons and comic strips from newspapers. Notice how each character looks in each section of a comic strip. Also notice how each of the character's words are often written inside a balloon.

2. You may find it helpful to create and sketch a cartoon or a comic strip on a piece of paper before you draw it on the sidewalk.

3. Have fun drawing your cartoon or comic strip on the sidewalk. If you draw a comic strip, use each section of the sidewalk to represent a section of the strip.

SIDEWALK COACH

**I can be a "Sidewalk Coach" when I teach others
to play a game on the sidewalk.**

HOW TO BE A SIDEWALK COACH

MATERIALS: Game books and whatever other supplies you may need.

SIDEWALK FUN:

1. Read about some games that you can play on a sidewalk, or better yet, create your own sidewalk games. Then choose a game to coach.

2. What is the object of your game? Practice how you are going to teach the game to others so that your directions will be clear when you do teach it.

3. Will you be an understanding and patient coach? Good Luck!

SIDEWALK DANCER

I can be a "Sidewalk Dancer" when I dance on the sidewalk.

HOW TO BE A SIDEWALK DANCER

MATERIALS: "Sidewalk Dancer" (music on page 67), music books with familiar tunes.

SIDEWALK FUN:

1. Learn the music and the actions for "Sidewalk Dancer."

2. Sing and dance to the "Sidewalk Dancer" on a sidewalk.

3. Create your own dance to a familiar tune. After you know how to do the dance well, teach it to others and perform it together on the sidewalk.

SIDEWALK DANCER

SIDEWALK ENTERTAINER

I can be a "Sidewalk Entertainer" when I tell people what I've learned to see and hear and do on the sidewalk.

HOW TO BE A SIDEWALK ENTERTAINER

MATERIALS: Sidewalk chalk, toy microphone (if you haven't made a toy microphone, see page 70, "How To Be A Sidewalk Musician" for directions.)

SIDEWALK FUN:

1. Practice what you are going to do as an entertainer. You might, for example, recite poetry, tell a story, dance, talk about an art display, explain a math activity, share your science observations, and/or sing a song.

2. This is your chance to share what you have learned about the things that you can do on or near a sidewalk. Remember to speak loudly and clearly so that everyone can hear you. Your audience will want to hear what you have to say.

3. Draw a circle to represent a spotlight circle. Then step into the circle and entertain your family and friends.

SIDEWALK MATHEMATICIAN

**I can be a "Sidewalk Mathematician"
when I do math on the sidewalk.**

HOW TO BE A SIDEWALK MATHEMATICIAN

MATERIALS: Measuring tapes or yard sticks, chalk, clipboard, pencil, paper.

SIDEWALK FUN:

1. Make a "start" line on the sidewalk with chalk. Walk a distance and make a "stop" line on the sidewalk. Estimate how far you think you have walked. Then measure the distance that you actually walked. Record both measurements on a sheet of paper.

2. Write math facts and work on math problems on the sidewalk.

3. Draw and label geometrical figures on the sidewalk.

4. Be creative! Think of other mathematical activities to do on the sidewalk.

SIDEWALK MUSICIAN

**I can be a "Sidewalk Musician" when I sing songs
in the spotlight on the sidewalk.**

HOW TO BE A SIDEWALK MUSICIAN

MATERIALS: "I'm A Star" (music on page 71), chalk, a toilet paper tube, newspaper, aluminum foil for making a toy microphone.

SIDEWALK FUN:

1. Make a toy microphone as shown in the illustration below:

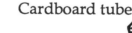

Newspaper with foil covering

Cardboard tube

2. Learn the song "I'm A Star."

3. Draw a large circle on the sidewalk to represent a spotlight circle.

4. Step inside the spotlight circle and sing other songs using your microphone.

I'M A STAR

If all the children are singing, substitute his/her or he's/she's.

SIDEWALK SCIENTIST

I can be a "Sidewalk Scientist" when I observe living things on or near the sidewalk and make a record of my discoveries.

HOW TO BE A SIDEWALK SCIENTIST

MATERIALS: Plastic magnifying glass (optional), clipboard, paper.

SIDEWALK FUN:

1. Stop, look, and listen to what you can discover on the sidewalk. Record your thoughts on paper about the things that you have observed.

2. Also include in your records what you see near the edge of the sidewalk.

3. Share the information that you learned about the living things on and near the sidewalk with your family and friends. Ask them what they have seen on or near the sidewalk.

SIDEWALK NEWS REPORTER

I can be a "Sidewalk Newspaper Reporter" when I write an article about the events that happen on or near the sidewalk.

HOW TO BE A SIDEWALK NEWSPAPER REPORTER

MATERIALS: Paper and pencil

SIDEWALK FUN:

1. Stop, look, and listen! What do you see, hear, smell, touch, and taste? Use your senses to get ideas for a newspaper article. Answer as many of the journalism questions (who? what? where? when? why? and how?) as you need for your article.

2. Take notes for your article. What do you want to say at the beginning, in the middle, and at the end of it?

3. After you have made plans for your article, write it as well as you can.

4. Reread your article to see that you have said what you want others to read. Check for spelling, capitalization, and punctuation.

5. Share your newspaper article with family and friends.

RESOURCES

ART

Arnosky, Jim. *Drawing From Nature*. New York: Lothrop, Lee and Shepard, 1987.

Arnosky, Jim. *Drawing Life in Motion*. New York: Lothrop, Lee and Shepard Books, 1984.

Greenberg, Jan and Sandra Jordon. *The Painter's Eye: Learning To Look at Contemporary American Art*. New York: Delacorte Press, 1991.

Hollingsworth, Patricia and Stephen. *Smart Art: Learning to Classify and Critique Art*. Tucson, Arizona: Zephyr Press, 1989.

Katz, Phyllis. *Exploring Science Through Art*. New York: Franklin Watts, 1991.

Kinghorn, Harriet and Lisa Lewis-Spicer. *Classic To Contemporary — Famous Artists and Activities*. Minneapolis, Minnesota: T.S. Denison, 1993.

Kinghorn, Harriet and Lisa Lewis-Spicer. *Let's Meet famous Artists*. Minneapolis, Minnesota: T.S. Denison, 1991.

Kohl, Mary Ann F. and Cindy Gainer. *Good Earth Art: Environmental Art For Kids*. Illus. by Cindy Gainer. Bellingham, Washington: Bright Ring Publishers, 1991.

Lancaster, John. *Cardboard*. Photography by Chris Fairclough. New York: Franklin Watts, 1989.

Lancaster, John. *Paper Sculpture*. Photography by Chris Fairclough. New York: Franklin Watts, 1989.

Lipman, Jean and Margaret Aspinwall. *Alexander Calder and His Magical Mobiles*. New York: Hudson Hills Press, 1981.

Raphael , Elaine and Don Bolognese. *Drawing History, Ancient Egypt*. New York: Franklin Watts, 1989.

Sibley, Brian. *The Pooh Sketchbook*. Drawings by Ernest H. Shepard for the Pooh stories by A.A. Milne. New York: E.P. Dutton, 1984.

Solga, Kim. *Art and Activities for Kids To Draw!* Cincinnati, Ohio: F&W Publications, 1991.

Tofts, Hannah. *The Print Book — Fun Things to Make and Do with Print*. New York: Simon & Schuster, 1990.

Tofts, Hannah. *The 3-D Paper Book — Fun Things to Make and Do with Paper*. New York: Simon & Schuster, 1990.

Ventura, Piero. *Great Painters*. New York: G.P. Putnam's Sons, 1984

Yenawine, Phillip. *Lines*. New York: Delacorte, 1991.

DRAMA

Adorjan, Carol and Yuri Rasovsky. *WKID: Easy Radio Plays*. Illus. by Ann Iosa. Niles, Illinois: Albert Witman and Company, 1988.

Alexander, Sue. *Small Plays for Special Days*. Illus. by Tom Huffman. Boston: Houghton Mifflin, 1979.

Ayckbourn, Alan. *Mr. A's Amazing Maze Plays*. Winchester, Maryland: Faber and Faber, 1990.

Bellville, Cheryl W. *Theatre Magic: Behind The Scenes At Children's Theatre*. Minneapolis, Minnesota: Carolrhoda, 1986.

Birch, Beverly. *Shakespeare's Stories: Comedies*. Illus. by Carol Tarrant. New York: P. Bedrick Books, 1988.

Boiko, Claire. *Children's Plays for Creative Actors*. Boston: Plays, 1985.

Brooks, Courtaney. *The Case of the Stolen Dinosaur: A Play in Two Versions: Stage and Radio*. Illus. by Merrilee Way. Manhattan Beach, California: Belnice Books, 1983.

Brooks, Courtaney. *Pardner and Freddie: A Puppet Play*. Illus. by Merrilee Way. Manhattan Beach, California: Belnice Books, 1983.

Bush, Max. *The Voyage of the Dragonfly*. New Orleans, Louisiana: Anchorage, 1989.

Chorpenning, Charlotte B. *The Adventure of Tom Sawyer*. Woodstock, Illinois: Dramatic Publishers, 1956.

Dahl. Roald. *Charlie and the Chocolate Factory*. Illus. by Joseph Schindelman. New York: Knopf, 1991.

Dunster, Mark. Chimney. *Hollywood*, California: Linden Publishing, 1990.

Fisher, Aileen. *Year-Round Programs for Young Players*. Boston: Plays, 1985.

Havilan, Amorie and Lyn Smith. *Easy Plays for Preschoolers to Third Graders*. Brandon, Mississippi: Quail Ridge, 1985.

Haycock, Kate. *Plays*. Ada, Oklahoma: Garrett Ed Corp., 1991.

Kline, Suzy. *The Herbie Joines Reader's Theatre*. Illus. by Richard Williams. New York: G.P. Putnam's Sons, 1992.

Rockwell, Thomas. *How To Eat Fried Worms: And Other Plays*. Illus. by Joel Schick. New York: Delacorte, 1980.

GAMES

Ball Games. Scarsdale, New York: Marshall Cavendish, 1990.

Benarde, Anita. *Games From Many Lands*. Illus. by Anita Benarde. Scarsdale, New York: Lion Books, 1990.

Buskin, David. *Outdoor Games*. Illus. by Dick Kline. Scarsdale, New York: Lion Books, 1966.

Cobb, Vicki. *How To Really Fool Yourself: Illusions for All Your Senses*. New York: HarperCollins Child Books, 1981.

Corbett, Pie. *Playtime Treasury*. New York: Doubleday, 1990.

Eberle, Bob. *Scamper On*. Illus. by June K. Weber. Buffalo, New York: DOK Publishers, 1984.

Elinon, Dorothy. *Play with a Purpose: Learning Games for Children Six Weeks to Ten Years*. Illus. by Jon Farndon. New York: Pantheon, 1986.

Greenaway, Kate. *Kate Greenaway's Books of Games*. New York: St. Martin, 1987.

Kalbfeisch, Susan. Jump! *The New Jump Rope Book*. Illus. by Laurie McGugan. New York: Morrow Junior Books, 1987.

Kalter, Joanmarie. *The World's Best String Games*. New York: Sterling, 1990.

Oakley, Ruth. *Chanting Games*. North Bellmore, New York: Marshall Cavendish, 1990.

Oakley, Ruth. *Games with Papers and Pencils.* North Bellmore, New York: Marshall Cavendish, 1989.

New Games Book: Play Hard, Play Fair, Nobody Hurt. Edited by Andrew Fluegelman. New York: Headlands Press Book, 1978.

Vecchione, Glen. *The World's Best Street and Yard Games.* New York: Sterling, 1989.

MUSIC AND MOVEMENT

Blumers, Charlotte and Jacques Rizzo. *Action Fun & Game Songs (For Kindergarten and Primary Classes).* Pennsylvania:Bryn Mawr, 1981.

Doll, Edna and Mary Jorman Nelson. *Rhymes Today!* Illus. by Laura Johnson. Morristown, New Jersey: Silver Burdett, Co., 1965.

Glazer, Tom. *Eye Winker, Tom Tinker, Chin Chopper: Fifty Musical Fingerplays with Piano Arrangements for Guitar Cords.* Illus. by Ron Himler. Garden City, New York: Doubleday, 1973.

Grier, Gene and Audry. *Sing, Dance, and Do: A Practical Approach to Singing in the Classroom.* Dayton, Ohio: The Heritage Music Press, 1989.

Kenney, Maureen. *Circle Round The Zero.* Photographs by Harriet Kiebanoff. St. Louis, Missouri: Magnamusic-Baton, Inc., 1975.

Nelson, Ester L. *Dancing Games for Children of All Ages.* Illus. by Shizu Matsuda. New York: Sterling Publishing Co., 1974.

Nelson, Ester L. *Musical Games for Children of All Ages.* Illus. by Shizu Matsuda. New York: Sterling Publishing Co., 1976.

Palmer, Hap. *Hap Palmer's Favorites: Songs for Learning Through Music and Movement.* Sherman Oaks, California: Alfred Publishing Co., 1981.

Palmer, Hap. *Songs to Enhance the Movement Vocabulary of Young Children.* Sherman Oaks, California: Alfred Publishing Co., 1987.

Palmer, Hap. *Turn on the Music. (Song and Activity Book).* Van Nuys, California: Alfred Publishing Co., 1989.

Pinzino, Mary Ellen. *Come Children Sing.* Illus. by Jeffrey and David Pinzino. Homewood, Illinois: Come Children, Sing, 1979.

Raffi. *Raffi Singable Songbook*. Illus. by Joyce Yamamoto. Don Mills, Ontario: Chappell, (n.d.).

Shatron, Lois and Bram. *Elephant Jam: A Trunkful of Musical Fun for the Whole Family*. New York: McGraw-Hill Ryerson Limited, 1980.

NUTRITIOUS SNACKS

Aber, Linda. *Stuck on Cooking*. New York: Scholastic Inc., 1991.

Better Homes & Gardens Editors. *New Junior Cookbook*. Des Moines, Iowa: Meredith Books, 1989.

Betty Crocker Staff, ed. *Betty Crocker's New Boys and Girls Cookbook*. New York: Betty Crocker, 1990.

Cobblestone Publishing, Inc. Staff. *Recipes From Around The World: For Young People 8 - 14*. Peterborough, New Hampshire: Cobblestone Publishing, 1987.

Coyle, Rena. *My First Cookbook*. Illus.. by Jerry Joyner. New York: Workman Publishers, 1985.

Macdonald, Kate. *The Anne of Green Gables Cookbook*. Illus. by Barbara DiLella. New York: Oxford University Press, 1987.

Moore, Marsha. *The Teddy Bear Book*. South Yarmouth, Maryland: A.D. Bragdon, 1984.

Parents Nursery School Staff. *Kids are Natural Cooks*. New York: Houghton Mifflin, 1974.

Paul, Aileen. *Kids' Cooking Without A Stove: A Cookbook for Young Children*. Illus. by Carol Inouye. Santa Fe, New Mexico: Sunstone Press, 1985.

Pemberton, Judy. *Let's Get Cooking*. Illus. by Judith Anderson. Phoenix, Arizona: King Fisher Press, 1984.

Sesame Street Cookbook. New York: Putnam Publishing Group, 1978.

Supraner, Robyn. *Quick and Easy Cookbook*. Illus. by Renzo Barto. Mahwah, New Jersey: Troll Associates, 1981.

Van der Linde, Polly and Tasha. *Around the World in Eighty Dishes*. Illus. by Horst Lemke. Merrick, New York: Scroll Press, 1971.

Wolfe, Bob and Diane. *Holiday Cooking Around the World*. Photographs by Diane Wolfe. Illus. by Jeannette Swofford. Minneapolis, Minnesota: Lerner Publications, 1988.

Zweifel, Frances W. *Pickle in the Middle and Other Easy Snacks*. Illus. by Frances Zweifel. New York: HarperCollins Children's Books, 1979.

SIDEWALKS AND CAREERS

Arnosky, Jim. *Drawings From Nature* New York: Lothrop, 1987.

Cheatham, Val R. *Cartooning for Kids Who Draw & Who Don't Draw*. Buffalo, New York: DOK, 1976.

Cox, Phil. *Fragment of a Sidewalk*. Illus. by Ed Rayher. Amherst, Maryland: Swamp Press, 1986.

Fitz Gerald, C. *I Can Be A Reporter*. Chicago: Childrens Press, 1986.

Hankin, Rebecca. *I Can Be A Musician*. Chicago: Childrens Press, 1984.

Hirsch, Linda. *You're Going Out There a Kid, but You're Coming Back a Star*. Illus. by John Wallner. New York: Bantam, 1984.

Hoban, Tana. *I Walk and Read*. New York: Greenwillow, 1984.

Kemsley, James. *The Cartoon Book*. New York: Scholastic, 1991.

Nelson, Patricia. *There's a Hole in My Sidewalk*. Alburtis, Pennsylvania: Stoneback, 1977.

Silverstein, Shel. *Where The Sidewalk Ends*. New York: HarperCollins Child Books, Inc., 1974.

Storms, Laura. *Careers with an Advertising Agency*. Illus. by Milton J. Blumfield. Minneapolis, Minnesota: Lerner Publications, 1984.

Tolan, Stephanie. *Sophie and the Sidewalk Man*. Illus. by Susan Avishai. New York: Macmillan Child Group, 1992.

Wake, Susan. *Advertising*. Ada, Oklahoma: Garrett Ed Group., 1991.

Zeck, Gerry. *I Love To Dance*. Minneapolis, Minnesota: Carolrhoda, 1982.